Girl Get It Right!

Girl Get it Right!

An I.M.P.A.C.T. guide to creating the life
and work you dream of

Gayle Guest-Brown

Girl Get it Right!

An I.M.P.A.C.T. guide to creating the life and work you dream of

Copyright @ 2018 Gayle Guest-Brown.

Books are available for purchase on Amazon.com and directly from the author on her website. www.guestbrownimpact.com

Because of the dynamic nature of the Internet, URLs, links or web addresses contained in this book may change after publication of this book.

Cover Artist
SelfPubBookCovers.com/DesignzbyDanielle

ISBN-13: 978-1727358919

ISBN-10:1727358910

Publication date: October 2018

Shannon ~
You were such
a blessing to work with
Peace Sis!
[signature]

DEDICATION

Ladies, this one's for you!

I believe women are God's gift to this world. We are incredibly resilient and resourceful. Women gave birth to humanity, and yet we are often undervalued and our true essence, beauty, and strength are unappreciated. Humanity benefits when women understand and access the power within them, align their actions with their values, and are fully supported, as women are integral to the healthy functioning of families. Families impact communities, which in turn impact cities, which in turn impact states, countries, and the world.

TABLE OF CONTENTS

FOREWORD

As a friend to Gayle for 21 years and husband for 14 years, I've enjoyed a front row seat to Gayle's impressive transformation. I've watched many times (and occasionally joined her) as she creates something impactful from nothing. It's drawn me to her. To quote that familiar Commodores lyric, *"How can she lose with the stuff she use."* [i] Faith, boldness, humility, and tenacity…get some for yourself. It's all in here. Then hang on, like I have, for the wild and wonderful ride of your life!

Ernest W. Brown

Engineer, Violence Prevention and Personal Finance Advocate

CONTRIBUTORS

I gratefully acknowledge all the contributors and helpers that aided in bringing this book to fruition.

Editor: The patient and thorough **Christina Files** at christina.e.files@gmail.com | www.christinafiles.com

My husband, **Ernest Winston Brown**, for all the editing, loving support, and for suggesting the title of this book!

Contributing Artists

Chapters 1, 3
The brave and talented, **Rachel Brewer** | brewer1792@gmail.com

Chapters 2, 6
Marleece Peart | marleece@mpdesigns.2012.com
MP Designs creates products such as transformative art, jewelry, and accessories.

Chapter 5
Alex Piedra, Davis California

Closing
Victoria Nenneman Ritter | mnvr55@hotmail.com

Last but not least, much gratitude to my writing group, the **River Rock Writers** who nurtured me a and inspired me to write. They edited the very first draft of this manuscript.

I thank you with all my heart for helping me with this project and enabling a dream to come true. My God bless you ten fold!

No matter your issue or challenge, the inspiring action steps I suggest can help you bounce back, recover, and thrive!

—Gayle Guest-Brown

PREFACE

Over the years, as a manager of people, a ministry leader, peer counselor, and now as a leadership coach, I have spoken with hundreds of women who long for another life, another job, another husband. They want more! More happiness, more peace, more balance, more respect. They wanted to be fully seen, fully heard, and fully valued. I have a heart for women, and they have been my focus for the last twenty years. It's not that men wouldn't benefit from following these steps, because they would. This book, however, was written with my sisters in mind.

While this book contains vignettes based on my life, it is not a memoir. If titillating details of life gone awry is what you are looking for, there are many stories already on the market to choose from. This book is about how to prevail over your circumstances. The aim is to inspire and motivate. Until now, I could only reach those within the sound of my voice. This book allows me to expand my impact to include those across the world who would reach for help in a book. The purpose of this book is to impart hope, encouragement, and strategies to help you press toward your dreams.

My life's purpose is to *be a beacon to others on the path to living peacefully, joyfully, and on purpose!* With this offering, I am walking out the purpose and vision for my life. May you be inspired to do likewise.

I want to honor and thank those who have helped me in pursuit of my dream. First and foremost, my God, who has been so patient in the pursuit of my heart and so faithful in His love and provision for me. My Husband, Ernest Winston Brown, a man of character whom I adore and treasure. You brought music and dancing back into my life. Hugs to my amazing family, friends, and my ancestors. I am the dreams of my ancestors, and I called on their strength, perseverance, and resiliency to make it through the downturns of my journey. My ancestors left a 200-year legacy of values for God, education, community, and entrepreneurship.

INTRODUCTION

My heart throbbed wildly as I stood in court before the judge, my husband, his attorney, the entire courtroom, and God. I stood alone, fingering the pages of my four-page Victim Impact report. My mood was somber. It was a funeral of sorts. This action would surely be the nail in the coffin of my marriage. I wished I had brought someone for support, but it was too late now. I was there to testify against my husband and plead that he remain in custody. Earlier, I listened to the court docket as many women pleaded with the judge to release their husbands from jail. They minimized their husband's attacks and betrayal of trust so that their husbands could return to work and provide for their families. I knew that most women would not go to court and testify against their husbands, and that weighed heavily on my heart. I had been struggling with supporting him, as he battled addiction, and taking care of myself. My heart was torn, I needed to separate from him for my own safety and well-being. My head and my spirit, however, knew what must be done.

"Your honor, it gives me no pleasure to be here today." My voice faltered and then steadied. *"As I see it, it is a matter of self-preservation. If he is allowed to post bail, I believe my life is in imminent danger."*

I didn't look up. I couldn't look up. Embarrassed to admit this in open court, I continued on recounting the dates, details of his attacks, the injuries, the fear, his escalating drug abuse, the time I had missed from work, and my leave of absence from my graduate degree program. I shared only the most relevant of the unspeakable secrets of our lives. Publicly testifying to such intimate matters was humiliating and the latest low in our marriage and my life. I was and still am very image conscious. This was a sad day. I spoke my truth that day. I chose Me, my safety, and my peace. The costs were high: his incarceration, a failed marriage, broken hearts, and financial devastation, but the value I had for my life was worth this price. The threat of losing it made it even more precious. I loved him but I loved me too!

Many women in these situations experience a war between their head and their heart. Many of the socially constructed gender norms circulated in my thoughts as I stood in court like, "stand by your man," "you can't leave a sick man" (addiction is an illness), and I felt the added pressure of the social norm that puts more responsibility on a woman to keep a marriage together. My own mother was worried about appearances; in her mind, it was better to be married than to be divorced. I later learned that my family would filter my divorce through a lens of their dreams, aspirations, and expectations for me. My family was well meaning, but I could not add the additional burden of their expectations and dreams to the war I was already battling internally. They were not living my nightmare. My spirit knew what to do. On this day, my spirit would lead, my head would drive, and my heart would take the back seat.

As I left the courtroom that day, I had no idea where my life was heading. I knew only that my heart was now aching and would need a long time to heal and recover from the loss of someone I loved dearly and the traumatic events described that day in Court 62. That was 20 years ago.

Here's the good news. It is never too late to begin again and to create a new reality. Life is full of twists and turns, and sometimes, you might just find yourself broken up and sidelined, wondering if this is all you get out of life. I know that feeling well. I am a living witness that we get more than one chance to figure out this journey called life. I have reinvented myself at least three times for various reasons. Today, I am wonderfully remarried to a man who loves and honors me. I am happy, in love, and doing the work I love, work that is life-changing for my clients and has served to refuel me. This I.M.P.A.C.T. guide is comprised of the most effective actions and tactics I have used to create the life, the love, and the work I dreamed of. You may face different and difficult circumstances, but I believe you too can improve your situation.

In the winter of 1998, I was picking up the remnants of a ten-year marriage that had become unhinged. A marriage wrecked by our self-involved lifestyle. We were enjoying life, partying and traveling, until it spiraled into his drug abuse (self-inflicted harm) and eventually into domestic violence (emotional and physical harm inflicted on me). The marriage that seemed magical for five years was over.

I ignored my aching heart because it just couldn't be trusted. It was still very much in love with a man that had become addicted to drugs and who was sometimes tender but most often reckless and violent. I mustered the strength to step into the unknown and start a new life. Among other things, I left behind a beautiful, cedar-shingled, 3000-square-foot home and transitioned to a quiet, one-and-a-half-bedroom, 700-square-foot apartment. This move felt like a step backwards, but this little apartment was filled with light and there was a lot of peace there. The peace in that quiet apartment was treasured; this space would become my respite. A setback in life may require occupying less space for a while and having fewer things. I found the trade-off of material things for peace and safety a good one. You can live simply and still have comfort. This was how the season of taking stock and of coming back to myself began.

My life was in pieces around my ankles. My husband at the time was in jail on three felony counts of abusive behavior. My forever and ever, amen dreams were shattered. My heart was broken, my future was unclear, and I was emotionally sick to the point of numbness.

I was doing the hard work of starting over, going through the motions at work, and finishing a graduate degree at U.C. Davis. My head was functioning, but my heart was broken. I could not allow myself to feel, not for a while. I put my hand in God's hand and lived one step at a time and one day at a time until eventually the pain and confusion subsided, and I was able to feel joy again. Life was uncertain at first, but step by step and day by day it was being transformed. Walking away from my marriage began the hardest two years of my life and felt like walking through hell, but those two years were the road to my ultimate deliverance and freedom. It was all part of the healing process on the path to the incredible life I have today and have been living for the last 15 years.

Feel free to read "higher power" whenever I reference God or Jesus. It's okay if our stories do not align in every way, but my God was so instrumental in my transition I wouldn't dare deny him now. My God was a 24/7 friend. I didn't always have what I wanted, but I had the basic things I needed.

Mine is a story of overcoming domestic violence and divorce. Your obstacle and challenges may be different, but there are lessons here for you. No matter your issue or challenge, the inspiring action steps I suggest can help you bounce back, recover from life's setback and thrive. By the way, setbacks are more common than you think. It's how you bounce back that matters. You must get up and begin again. I used the word setback purposefully. It is a neutral word and does not assign blame. It does not matter if you fell down or you were pushed, the process to recovery is the same. You simply must get up and begin again.

In the following pages, you will find inspirational quotes, scriptures, bits and pieces of my story to inspire you, and action steps to motivate you to start your own journey. These actions align with the acronym I.M.P.A.C.T., and they will have an impact on your life, as you apply them. Each chapter contains three or four action verbs to activate your best life. Taking action, changing your mindset, and moving your feet is the only way to achieve your dreams. You cannot stay where you are and move into your future. My hope and prayer are that you will be inspired to START TODAY to have the life you envision tomorrow.

Welcome to the *Girl Get it Right!* I.M.P.A.C.T. Guide!

Girl Get it Right!

These six chapters, a chapter for each of the six letters in the acronym I.M.P.A.C.T., will help you tap into your strengths, align your values, catch your vision, and begin pursuing your dreams.

*I*magine • *Initiate* • *Illuminate*

*M*editate • *Move* • *Manifest*

*P*lan • *Prepare* • *Premeditate* • *P.U.S.H.*

*A*lign • *Affirm* • *Authenticate*

*C*ultivate • *Communicate* • *Connect*

*T*ransition • *Transform* • *Transcend*

Chapter 1

Unleash Your Dreams

"If my mind can conceive it, and my heart can believe it, then I can achieve it."

—Muhammad Ali[ii]

"For I know the plans I have for you," declares the Lord, "plans to prosper you and not to harm you, plans to give you hope and a future."

Jeremiah 29:11 NIV

"Just because the past didn't turn out like you wanted it to, doesn't mean your future can't be better than you ever imagined it."

—Ziad K. Abdelnour
Author & Investment Banker

Action: *Imagine • Initiate • Illuminate*

Imagine

Every life journey has a beginning, a middle, and an end. Somewhere before your endpoint you want to be living the life of your dreams. Where do you want to go? What are your dreams for your life? Your dream is what you picture in your mind's eye, that Utopia, that ideal state that makes your heart smile. Hint: If your vision doesn't fire your soul, then you are probably dreaming too small. It can be a sign that you have work to do in unseating limiting beliefs about who you are or what you can achieve. I believe so much more is possible than we sometimes give ourselves credit for. Some of you may have had numerous challenges in life which can erode confidence and will power in some instances. It's okay to consult with a therapist or a life coach if you are having trouble believing in yourself.

Why not reach for your biggest, wildest daydream? You may have hidden your dreams from others, but your dreams are there, deep in your soul. In this chapter, you will begin with the end in mind. You will begin to create your future by visualizing it. You will imagine it!

I love the quote by Hal Elrod, author of *Miracle Morning*. He says, *"Where you are is a result of who you were, but where you go depends entirely on who you choose to be, from this moment on."*

"Your imagination is your preview of life's coming attractions."

—Albert Einstein

My Story Circa 2010: *The Courage to Imagine*

I caught my vision one Saturday afternoon at Arco Arena in Sacramento. My sister bought a ticket for me to the Women of Faith Conference in

Sacramento, a mega Christian women's conference and it was my first. I was excited! On the stage sat a group of speakers and authors who were all white: there were no women of color whatsoever. No Blacks, Asians, or Latinos. I was annoyed that this conference didn't assemble a panel of diverse women at an event in California, a state known as a cultural melting pot! Really! After seven years at Toastmasters, I knew that speakers usually consider their audience. What were they thinking?
I enjoyed their stories, but the still quiet voice inside of me said, *"You could be up there."* I thought that it looked like a cool gig: spreading hope and encouragement to thousands of women a day. Then the doubts crept in. Who was I kidding? I wasn't a published author! After the conference, I went on with my life. I would occasionally remember that tug on my heart. That tug to reach a larger audience with my own message of encouragement and of overcoming great adversity.

My journey would twist and turn, but I believed that vision to be a part of my destiny. The path hasn't always been easy but it has been purposeful. I have been falling forward into my future. All ports along my life's journey were simply preparing me for my destiny. I believe in the adage that you don't have to see the whole staircase to take the first step. I just kept consulting my God. I keep trusting and believing. I kept going!

Today, I am a published author and speak to hundreds of women across the nation! Well, really just California and Texas, but I'm not done yet. I am actually walking in the life I dreamed of!

One of the things that encouraged me was compiling a simple list. I am urging you to do this as well. The purpose of this exercise is to reconnect to your body, heart, and soul. Today the reconnection begins. Your new journey begins with you! Only you can chart that path. Allowing yourself to dream and imagine is a first step! Albert Einstein, once said, *"Imagination is more important than Knowledge."*

Let yourself imagine the possibilities. The following exercises will help you get started.

Exercise I: 50 Things that Make You Smile on the Inside

This exercise is not to intended to be completed in the moment or a day. The request is to list 50 things that make you smile on the inside, 50 things that make your heart happy!

In the rush and hub-bub of life, we become disconnected from the joys of our heart. You will be surprised how hard it is to come up with fifty unique items. My list included hearing the crashing waves at the beach, seeing a glorious sunset, biting into a red candied apple, and so on. You can complete your list over a week or two. Just the thought of reconnecting to these long-lost friends, memories, thoughts, and smells will help your heart soar.

You may not be aware of how life's ups and downs have impacted you. If you're having a hard time dreaming or life has beaten you up a bit, this exercise can help restore your sense of wonderment and awe, which will in turn prepare you to dream about your future.

To treat yourself, for kicks, or for inspiration, check out *"150 Often Overlooked Blessings"* by Sarah Be Breathnach[1]

If you are going to take the time to start your life anew, you might as well populate it with what makes your heart smile. It was during this exercise that salsa dancing and trips to the beach re-entered my life. In the second half of my life, getting to the beach and dancing have become a central part of life. I had always wanted to ski, so I joined the local ski club and learned to ski. I also gained a whole new circle of friends who shared my interest.

So, you know those hobbies and interests you enjoy but never find the time to do? Add those things to your list. It's your list, it's your life, and it's the only one you get!

As you take time to imagine what you want in your new life, be sure to sprinkle your vision with items from this list. After you have completed your list, take the next step and give yourself permission to imagine the life you want. This holistic view should encompass your mind, body, soul, and spirit. I encourage you to think expansively about work, recreation, people, and places. Allow yourself to initiate new practices as you incorporate people and things that are aligned with making your heart sing.

Exercise II: Visioning (Time required: 2 Hours or 15 mins/day for 8 days)

Creating a visual reminder of what exactly you are moving toward can be a great motivator to keep you moving despite the trials. Vision boards are my go-to tool for this. Many of you may have vision boards already. If so, consider creating a new one focused on your new destination. If you have never created a vision board, this is a great time to try it.

If you are anything like me, you will believe you do not have enough time to do such a seemingly frivolous activity. If this is your thinking, may I suggest that you break the task into small sections and take 15 minutes a day, every day, for 10-15 days. Dreaming about your future is not frivolous and will yield great fruit in your life. Your imagination will make the possible visible

A vision board is a collection of images, magazine clippings, and words that you desire in your life.. As you take time to imagine what you want in your new life, be sure to sprinkle your vision with items from the *50 Things that Make your Heart Happy* list. Once you catch your vision, bring it to life with pictures. You will need a stack of old magazines, scissors, a glue stick, colored pencils, markers, colored construction paper, and a large 16x20 poster board. Next, create a sacred place to let your heart soar: play soft music or nature sounds, such as crashing waves. Set aside uninterrupted time. Look through magazines for images and words that you desire in your life. You may choose to draw what you do not find in magazines.

After you have put the finishing touches on your vision board, place the board where you can see it each morning. Scan each image and really visualize your dream. Allow yourself to step into it, one image at a time. Imagine what it would feel like to be that, to have that, in your life. Sense what it would feel like to experience it. Spend 10 minutes a day meditating on your vision board. It is a daily reminder of the life you are destined to lead. Having a clear picture of what you are moving toward in your life sets your intentions and attracts the opportunities to realize your dreams.

"Without Vision, the People Perish…"

Proverbs 29:18

"They always say time changes things, but you actually have to change them yourself"

—Andy Warhol
Artist, Author and Producer

INITIATE

One day, upon hanging up the phone with a close friend, wherein I complained fervently about the situation with my ex-husband, I realized that if I wanted a different life, I would have to do something different. I'd grumbled about my situation to friends and family for months, and then it came to me. **They** couldn't help me! My ex-husband had conflated his drug use with a bipolar diagnosis and he played on my helping tendencies. He would manipulate my emotions like a master conductor. One week he would play on my sympathy for his plight, and the next week he would take advantage of my desire to save our marriage. One day, it became clear as a bell. No one could help me. If I truly wanted to extricate myself from this downward spiral of a life, **I** would have to do it. I would have to do it for myself! Now I ask you, What are you complaining about to your friends? The future is yours to take.

The next day, I took one step and God took ten. My first step was going to a codependents anonymous support group. Each journey begins with the first step. So, lean into it. Go for it. Move through the fear. Run through the uncertainty. Trust in your higher power. Trust in your resilience. Just start to move away from what you do not want and towards something more! You may have to leave people and things behind. It's okay. **Just Start!**

> *"It will never rain roses; when we want to have more roses, we must plant more roses."*
>
> —George Eliot
> Poet and Playwright

> *"Rise up; this matter is in your hands. We will support you, so take courage and do it"*
>
> Ezra 10:4

"The best way to not feel hopeless is to get up and do something. Do not wait for good things to happen to you. If you go out and make some good things happen, you will fill the world with hope, and you will fill yourself with hope."

—Barack Obama
44th President of the USA

ILLUMINATE

To illuminate means to light up, to magnify, to brighten or cast light on. Changes require bold moves. We are going to take those dreams buried deep in you and bring them forward, so you can see, touch, and feel them. Let's celebrate the vision. Get your vision board. Frame it. Think on it. Meditate on it. Breathe in your hopes and dreams. Dare to believe.

"Nothing can dim the light which shines from within."
—Maya Angelo
Poet, Author, Activist

Happiness can be found in the darkest of times if one only remembers to turn on the light.
—J.K. Rowlings
Author of *Harry Potter and the Prisoner of Azkaban*

"When Jesus spoke again to the people, he said, 'I am the light of the world. Whoever follows me will never walk in darkness but will have the light of life.'"
John 8:12

Gratitude unlocks the goodness of life. We often overlook small blessings, but not during this time of transition. Elevate them! Illuminate them! Being thankful for what we already have opens the door for more.

Exercise III: Your Gratitude Journal

Keeping a Gratitude Journal really helped me keep my thoughts positive. It's a great way to start your day! I recommend keeping your journal next to your bed. Upon rising, start your day recording all the things that you are thankful for. Even the small things. Especially the small things. For example, the smell of fresh bread baking or the feel of fresh linen, a great night of sleep, whatever makes your heart smile.

My Story Circa 1998: *Turning on the Light*

My life was at its lowest point when I started keeping my gratitude journal. My estranged husband was out of jail and he held me responsible for putting him there, creditors were calling night and day to collect their debt from our once two-income household, and I was lonely.

You won't understand this if you've never had an obsessive man fixated on getting you back. My estranged husband would call often to convince me that I needed to come home if he was ever going to heal. Between him and the credit collectors, the phone had become an object of disdain.

It was hard for me, at that time, to think of something to be grateful for. The first day, I just looked at the page. Then, I began with the small things: a safe place to lay my head; a full-time, good-paying job; my friends; my church; singing in the choir. With all that was wrong, there were actually good things happening, too. Keeping a journal reminded me of the good things, opened my heart, and grounded me in that reality ever morning. This practice of writing daily in my gratitude journal helped me remain hopeful. You don't have to be going through a hard time to gain the benefits of gratitude. Forbes Magazine listed 7 scientifically proven benefits of gratitude: improved physical and psychological health, enhanced empathy and reduction in aggression, better sleep and improved self-esteem.[vi]

If you are in doubt about the benefits, just try it for one week and check in with yourself. Writing in your journal doesn't change your circumstances, but it can change your mindset, which can then change your circumstances. Change your mindset, change your life.

"Gratitude unlocks the fullness of life. It turns what we have into enough and more. It turns denial into acceptance, chaos to order, confusion to clarity. It can turn a meal into a feast, a house into a home, a stranger into a friend. Gratitude makes sense of the past, brings peace for today, and creates a vision for tomorrow."
—Melody Beattie
Author of *The Language of Letting Go*

Chapter 2

Take the Next Step

"The man who moves a mountain begins by carrying away small stones."

—Chinese proverb

"Start where you are you, use what you have, and do what you can."

—Arthur Ashe
Tennis Champion, Activist

"If it doesn't challenge you, it won't change you."

—Fred DeVito
Executive Vice President of Mind-Body Training

"Therefore we do not lose heart. Though outwardly we are wasting away, yet inwardly we are being renewed day by day. For our light and momentary troubles are achieving for us an eternal glory that far outweighs them all. So we fix our eyes not on what is seen, but on what is unseen, since what is seen is temporary, but what is unseen is eternal."

2 Corinthians 4:16-18

Action: *Meditate • Move • Manifest*

MEDITATE

To meditate means to focus your mind on a thought, on an object, or on silence. I'm advocating that you meditate silently. Meditation has a long tradition of bringing together the mind, body, and spirit; its benefits include focus, clarity, and alignment. Who doesn't need that? It's particularly important as you strive to create new ways of being. In the early days of my reinvention, I found it difficult to quiet my mind. I couldn't sleep, there were so many loose ends, my life was messy, and my soul was restless. My therapist made a seven-minute meditation and deep breathing tape for me to listen to every night and anytime I felt overwhelmed. It worked for me, when I took the time to do it.

In our busy lives, we do not spend time alone with our thoughts. It is even rarer to just be. My best friend Bonnie would tell me, *"Gayle, you are always doing. It is okay to Just Be."* She even modeled it for me. She taught me how to just go to the beach, relax, and do nothing. To sit in the glory and rhythm of waves crashing on the shore. Bonnie took a substantial vacation every quarter. She clearly valued travel to foreign destinations. She showed me how to live, laugh, and travel in the aftermath of a major life shift. To this day, the beach is where I go to recover from busyness when I'm feeling overwhelmed.

Sometimes, we can't hear the still quiet voice within us because we are so busy doing. I am still busy, but I have learned that when I take time to "just be," I feel better and my mind is more aligned and appreciative of my spirit and body. In those hectic early days of transition, I began by blocking out one day a month on my calendar. If someone invited me to something on that date, I would tell people I already had plans on that day. I didn't tell them I planned to do nothing. Radical, right? It was for me. I absolutely needed that time to breathe, think, rest, and *just be*. I still do this today when life gets demanding.

Hint: This is a great new practice to incorporate. It doesn't cost you anything and the benefits are innumerable.

Of course, you don't have to go to the beach to find peace within you. You can create a tranquil space in your home where you can do just that. Is there somewhere you can go to have an uninterrupted 10 to 15 minute to just be? Will you create a corner, a closet, an area where you can listen, be still, allow yourself to connect to your higher power, and yield to your higher power's wisdom.

Say yes to being with your thoughts. Your mind holds a lifetime of wisdom, if only you would access it and apply it. You may find it interesting to learn that mice exposed to two hours of silence per day developed new cells in the hippocampus, a region of the brain associated with memory, emotion, and learning. Silence and quiet times were important tools on my recovery journey.

My ASK: Will you create a new daily habit of spending 10 minutes in silence, meditation, or prayer?

MOVE

Even before we know all the details about our journey and our destination, we must step out in faith. Can we trust that our God (or higher power) can guide, protect, and provide for us? Once you have an inkling of the direction you want to pursue, begin to move toward it. You can't stay where you are and walk in the life of your dreams. You must move forward, one foot in front of the other. Then, keep moving, breathing, and dreaming.

For two years, I woke up daily to a very uncertain future. One of my constant and comforting affirmations was, "My uncertain future is safe in the hands of an all-knowing God." I stepped out in faith, and my God proved to be a faithful, constant ally, making a way when I could not see a path forward. In the beginning, I couldn't always hear his voice, but I did trust he had a plan. Knowing God comes through experiencing him. He speaks through the Holy Spirit, prayer, scripture, and circumstances. I would come to know him more intimately in these difficult times.

Was I afraid for tomorrow? Yes, at first I was. We can move forward through the fear. You **must** move through the fear to reach the other side.

It's been said that, "There is no fulfillment in life without risk." If you are having difficulty mustering the courage to move forward or to fall forward, borrow the courage of a friend. No friends? Get a therapist. Get creative. Inspirational speaker Iyanla Vanzant said, *"If you can't walk through the door, crawl through the window."* You, your life, and your dreams are worth it!

I penned the following poem many years after my divorce at another erratic time in my work life. I was digging myself out of what seemed to be a deep hole. It was dark in that hole, and I was working with many unknowns in a hostile environment. I applied all of my intellect, efforts, and spirit to the job at hand to no avail. You may wonder, what happened? Does it really matter? I use metaphor to protect the innocent. The details aren't the important part. The lesson, now that's what is important! Lesson: when you are in a hole, stop digging. Crawl out and begin again. I kept putting one foot in front of the other. I kept moving. I kept showing up and doing my part. Obstacles come to grow us and prepare us for our future.

Lesson: When you are in a hole, stop digging. Crawl out and begin again. I kept putting one foot in front of the other. I kept moving. I kept showing up and doing my part. Obstacles come to grow us and prepare us for our future.

The Path Forward

The path forward has many twists and turns
Sometimes it has switchbacks,
and yet, as long as it turns back in the direction we were headed,
it is still the path forward
The path forward has mountains and valleys and
it is still the path forward...if you keep moving.
The path forward has sunshine and rain
it may even storm
And it is still the path forward.
The path will most assuredly have joy and pain
and yet forward we go.
It will contain seasons of arduous work and time for rest and play,
if we remember to breathe.
The path forward consists of many well-intentioned steps
AND crap happens, and harm is done.
It is still the path forward
if we remember to breathe, make amends and keep moving.
We have everything we need to tackle the mountains ahead of us
on the path forward.

—Gayle Guest-Brown

Manifest

The Oxford Dictionary defines *manifest* as: to show (a quality or feeling) by one's acts or appearance; demonstrate. "Ray *manifested* signs of severe depression." The Merriam Webster dictionary defines *manifest* as: readily perceived by the senses and especially by the sense of sight. My practical definition of *manifest* is to bring forward.

I like this thought of manifesting your vision: to walk it out, to demonstrate it, to make it visible. I have done it at least three times.

Once, I joined the local black ski club and wondered why a club with a mission to place more African American downhill racers in the Olympics did not have a youth race team. I formed a committee that went on to research, recruit, and gain support from the club to fund a youth ski racing team. My current husband and I put a plan in place and ran the program for eight years. Every other weekend during the ski season, we would take children of color to the mountains for the weekend and teach them how to ski and race. The youth racing team was a vision manifested for us as well as our ski club. In 2006 we received the National Brotherhood of Skiers' (NBS) Mission Award in honor of our effort. Some of the team accomplishments include:

- One 2006 USSA Far West Team Member
- Two 2008 USSA Far West All-Academic Team Members
- One NBS National Team Member
- Six NBS Western Region Team Members
- Two USSA Certified Ski Coaches
- Thirteen athletes introduced to grassroots competition with six moving on to USSA competition

We dreamed about seeing a youth ski racing team for children of color, but walking that dream out brought about other dreams, too. As I worked on that project, I met a man who respected me and heard me. I worked alongside this man as he coached the team, and four years later we married. Meeting my husband wasn't part of my initial plan, but God knew my heart and he had a plan.

Next, I founded a Christian ministry to combat domestic violence in the faith community. That ministry, *From Bruised and Battered to Blessed* (BBB) was in place for 12 years to serve hundreds of women and youth. BBB Ministries also birthed Mixed Blessing, which was an intergenerational ministry providing education and awareness about teen dating violence. They went on to convene a 10-community agency collaboration to host a Sacramento's first Men of Integrity and Influence Conference targeting black men and boys to address men's roles in ending violence against women. This ministry and community work prepared me to step into the executive director role of a non-profit agency serving domestic violence and sexual assault victims. The director position was not part of my plan, but it was part of God's plan for my life.

The ministry manifested from a Women of Greatness conference I attended where the speaker encouraged attendees to "give birth to the seed God has placed in your belly." I knew she was speaking to me. I understood that to mean that God had destined me for great things and it was up to me to partner with Him in dreaming and walking out my personal destiny. I pictured God planting seeds of destiny in my soul that were ready to sprout new life in and through me. The previous year, I had ignored the spirit's quiet urging to do something about the silent epidemic of domestic violence, which had impacted me and so many of my friends. The day after the conference, I took a small step. I got a book on starting a ministry, and I began researching domestic violence. I found a plethora of resources out there. In time, I put a project plan in place and secured approval from my pastor.

Lastly, my life today is a manifestation of the thoughts and dreams I had way back in that little one-and-one-half bedroom apartment. My list of 50 things that make me smile on the inside included dancing, skiing, travel, flowers, and beaches. Today, my life is abundantly full of these very things. That is not an accident. I am amazed that my proudest accomplishments started with a single thought, which were then followed up with research, a plan, and then action. Isn't it magical that our thoughts impact our actions, which in turn physically manifest into our visions and a new reality? It does inspire confidence. I believe that most of us are capable of bringing their visions to life! I believe it is your duty to bring your dreams and your purpose to life. The universe is a waiting for you! As Iyala Vanzant says, *"No one can write your book, sing your song. It is your work to do."*

Take the first step, then the next. Don't forget to enjoy the journey and journal the journey. There are important lessons along the path to your destination. Trust me, you don't have to the know the ending to begin. **Just start.** Look around you...everything in the room began as a thought. Someone thought about it and produced it.

The Bible says, *"As a Man thinks, so he is"* (Proverbs 23:7). What you think about matters. So, do the exercises in Chapter One and think about what it is you want to create in your life. **Meditate** on it, **Move** toward it, and watch it **Manifest**!

I would love to hear your stories. Please take time now to connect with me and others on the path to creating the life and work they dream of on Facebook at the closed *Girl Get It Right! Action* Facebook Group.[ix]

"Tiptoe if you must, but take the first step!"
- Unknown

Chapter 3

Making the Invisible Visible

"Plans fail for lack of counsel, but with many advisers they succeed."

Proverbs 15:22

"Suppose one of you wants to build a tower, will not one sit down and estimate the cost to see if you have enough money to complete it?"

Luke 14:28

"A goal without a plan is just a wish."

—Antoine de Saint Exupery
French writer, poet, journalist, and pioneering aviator

Action: *Premeditate • Prepare • Plan • P.U.S.H.*

PREMEDITATE

"Someone's sitting in the shade today because someone planted a tree a long time ago."
—Warren Buffett
CEO Berkshire Hathaway, philanthropist

You have to seed the crop you want to harvest. Why not spend the time to image and envision your future? Now is the time to plant your fertile ground with the seeds of the crop you want to see and the trees you want to sit under in the future. So, how do we keep that ground fertile? Give your ideas room to grow. Shut out all negativity in the early season, and protect and nourish the seeds you planted. There is nothing quite as fragile as a new idea. Fertilize your crop and feed your soul.

What feeds your soul? For me, getting really close to God, studying scriptures, and singing in the choir fed my spirit during the season of transformation and rebirth. Simple things kept me going. Dancing and occasional trips to the beach fired my soul. Consider starting with your "50 Things that Make You Smile on the Inside" list. Haven't completed your 50 things? Why not pause and do that right now? **Follow-through is a key to success in life.**

My Story Circa 1999: *New Ways of Being*

At the brink of a new way of living, I recalled that dancing made my heart smile, and I definitely wanted more of it in my reinvented life. I heard about a local venue that had salsa dancing every Saturday night. I was not accustomed to going out alone. I was nervous about it. I wondered if would I be safe. The need to get out of my apartment and dance again drove me to go despite my fear. There was a part to me that felt downright unsafe, so I made this concession: I would go early and leave early. I would park close to the venue, in a well-lit parking space.

I would wear a smart compact bag with just identification, money, and lipstick. I would not take it off.

On Saturday, I dressed for the evening: black stretch pants with slight bell bottoms, complimented with a bright coral spaghetti-strap top. My hair gathered up on the top of my head in a short flume, along with dangly earrings. Salsa dancing could be very hot, depending on the ventilation. I looked in the mirror one last time. "You will be okay, "I said to the wide-eyed girl in the mirror and turned quickly and headed to the car. Well, I had a great time. This was a multi-generational gathering and whole families were there. The music was great! I was asked to dance, but no one bothered me for a phone number. They just wanted to dance! I felt safe and I was hooked!

After that, I started taking Salsa lessons! These classes eventually boosted my confidence. The added bonus was meeting a whole new circle of friends. All of us were beginning salsa dancers who loved and desired more dance in our lives. We began to plan outings to the local salsa dance clubs. We would look for each other when we were out and dance together. In less than a year, many of us were part of the local salsa dance scene. My girlfriend (also recently divorced) and I were going two nights a week. We told ourselves it was for the exercise. It was a nice way to have interactions with men without dating. I didn't want to date just yet. Years later, I would see my future husband many nights on the dance floor. Yes, he loved skiing and salsa dancing at least as much, if not more than, I did! Here's what I learned: <u>Do what you love.</u> When you meet someone doing what you love, you and your partner will have that in common. Whether you enjoy hiking, biking, gardening, skiing, or birdwatching, there is a club, class, or meetup group already meeting around that particular interest!

You know that thing you have wanted to do but never had time to do it? Now is the time! Just do it. **Start Today!** Go to www.meetup.com, Google, or Facebook and search for local groups doing what you love to do. Let's go!

PREPARE

Making the invisible visible starts with vision. That's the fun part. Visioning is followed by preparing, planning, and pushing.

My Story Circa 1995: *Using the Pain to Escape the Pain*

One sunny day in California, I was on the back porch, reading my mail alone. The bank statement had arrived. The day was perfect: not too hot, but a perfect 80 degrees with a gentle breeze. My ex-husband had just left mysteriously.

I looked at the Bank of America bank statement and again the savings account was depleted. It wasn't the money; this disappointment ran deeper than that. It was the death of a dream by a thousand not-so-little cuts. Where was this money going? I had just talked to him the month before and again the month before that. My then husband would look me in the eye, acknowledge me, and voice understanding of my concerns. He seemed uneasy. He had no explanation. I wasn't sure what exactly was happening. He'd confessed a bi-polar diagnosis, but this felt different than that. I'd asked him if he was doing drugs, but he denied this and would steer me to his confessed depression and bi-polar diagnosis. I learned that mental health medical information is heavily protected by HIPPA laws and spouses cannot can gain access to that information. My antenna was up, but I had remained hopeful until that day.

On that day, the numbers added up to: *Get the Hell Out! This was not a dream…it's a freaking nightmare!*

That was the day I surrendered the dream of saving my marriage and I began to strategically map my way out. I left the house and secured a P.O. Box. This would allow me to open a separate bank account and receive mail. I began to save money in this new account that was in my name only. That day I went apartment hunting. I signed up on several waiting lists. I listed my P.O. Box as a return address.

My path to freedom began with a P.O. Box. I don't know the exact day. I do know that with every future disappointment following the savings account incident, I would leverage my pain and hurt to make another step toward extracting myself from this sweet dream turned nightmare of a marriage. Our lives were enmeshed, and I knew this was not going to be easy. Still when a woman's done, she's done! Every day following "mail day," I woke up to a new and harsh reality. Mentally and emotionally preparing to leave your situation is the first step. If you have the luxury of time, spend some time thinking through your exit plan. You may be exiting a marriage, a relationship, an ill-fitting job, or be in a transition. Whatever the case, think through the next steps. Change and transition can be painful, so use the pain to motivate you toward your future and new circumstances.

> 'Give me six hours to chop down a tree and I will spend
> the first four hours sharpening the axe."
> —Abraham Lincoln

When charting a new trail, it is good to surround yourself with friends and advisors. The following worksheet is to help you build your support system. Take some time to fill in each block. Many of us have people in our lives we can trust. Be sure to communicate with them over the phone or coffee. Let them know you are on a new journey and will need their help. Solicit their confidential help as you begin your new life.

Note for domestic violence survivors: You may be isolated and have little outside contact beyond your relationship. In this case, it is important that you research local shelters. One resource is your local library. They have computers where you can search about domestic violence shelters in your county. These shelters can provide temporary housing for you. They will help you with safety planning and brainstorm with you about your options. Caution: Do not leave this list or book around if you are still living in an unsafe home. It could be hard to explain to an abusive partner or relative.

My Support System:

Note: This is a list of resource possibilities, you may not need or have access to all of these resources. Fill in names where you can or have need to.

	Name and Phone Number	Date Contacted
Exercise Partner		
Finances		
Legal		
Spiritual		
Taxes		
Business		
Personal/Career Coach		
Therapist		
Babysitter		
Other		

"By failing to prepare, you are preparing to fail."
—Benjamin Franklin

PLAN

*"Many are the plans in a person's heart, but it is the
Lord's purpose that prevails."*
—Proverbs 19:12

I love what Hal Elrod, author of *Miracle Morning*, says and I know it to be true. *"Setting goals is the first step in turning the invisible into the visible."* I do not know if planning is the <u>first</u> step, but it is certainly an important one!

So, now it's time to sit down and plan. I really recommend a great planner I was gifted in 2017 called a *"Passion Planner."* I have owned many planners, but I like that this one encouraged me to collect my dreams, goal reflections, and lessons learned in one place. It allowed me to break my goals down into smaller steps. If you are person who regularly plans, you will love it!

If you have never planned before, perhaps it's time to give it a try. One of the things differentiating this planner from others is that it provides a space for you to capture the lessons you learned from the previous month. Since you are on a new path, the ability to be able to go back and review what you learned from month to month is invaluable. If I were you, **I'd start today!**

To start planning, begin with the end in mind, then work backwards to lay out the steps to get there. Look at one goal at a time and break it down. Ask yourself, what steps can I take to move toward that goal?

Example:

Set SMART goals: Specific, Measurable, Reasonable, and Time specific.

Goal: Lose 20 pounds (a specific goal) by July 30th (A specific date)

The statement above is distinguished from a general and non-specific statement "I have a goal to lose weight."

SMART Goal Planned Action:

- Walk 30 minutes – 4 days/week – M, W, Th, Sat
- Eat salad for lunch 5 days/week
- Lift weights – 3 days/week – 20 minutes
- Salsa dance 2 times/week – 2 hours

If you have no idea about where to begin, what steps to take, go to the local bookstore or Google for help. YouTube has a variety of videos on various subjects. Be assured that in 6 million years of human civilization, someone else has dreamed the dream you have. In the book of Ecclesiastes, the scripture says: *"There is nothing new under the sun."*

> *"What has been will be again, what has been done will*
> *be done again; there is nothing new under the sun."*
> —Ecclesiastics 1:9

I am not saying this to diminish your ideas in any way. There is only one you, so whatever it is, it has not been done the way you would do it. You are uniquely gifted and no one can do things quite like you. However, you can learn from others who have done similar things, which will help you get started faster.

What if Steve Jobs said to himself, *"Well, Nokia already makes a pretty good cell phone,"* and let that stop him from producing the iPhone. What if Maya Angelou said to herself, *"Well, there already enough poems celebrating women out there,"* and "Phenomenal Woman" had not been written? **The world is waiting for you to do what only you can do!**

P.U.S.H.-Pray Until Something Happens

Or Persist Until Something Happens

There is great strength in connecting to a power bigger than yourself on this journey called life, particularly during times of transition and transformation.

Personally, I believe in the power of prayer, and I believe that prayer changes things. The Bible teaches us to pray without ceasing. For me, prayer is the way that I release my own will and connect to the supernatural power of the Lord. It is reassuring to know that I can communicate with the Creator of the Universe 24 hours a day, seven days a week. God was available when I awoke in the wee hours of the night. Yes, He was even present during the restless and anxious days of uncertainty. I could always lift a prayer to access the power available to me and the heavenly realm. While in the throes of a contentious and contested divorce, I would often call on church members or a prayer circle to intercede on my behalf. I wanted to be covered under a veil of prayer in the hardest times, and I was blessed to have a church family. God cares about the little problems as well. The Bible says, *"Do not be anxious about anything, but in every situation, by prayer and petition, with thanksgiving, present your requests to God. And the peace of God, which transcends all understanding, will guard your hearts and your minds in Christ Jesus."* (Philippians 4:6-7 NIV)

My Story Circa 1996: *The Magic of Prayer*

One particular evening, I was feeling extremely lonely. My apartment became my safe place. It was comfortable, and its second floor location provided a lot of light streaming through its high ceilings. There was a lot of peace in that little apartment and yet, I was just so lonely. I had chosen to isolate myself, because my life had become an embarrassment.

This was an self-imposed isolation. I didn't feel ready to address all the questions others would ask about the direction of my life. I was working by day and going to graduate school by night. When I did have a free day, joy was absent. I cried out to God, "Lord, I appreciate this space for my healing, but on this particular evening I am just so lonely! There has to be more!" I exclaimed, not believing there could be more in that moment.

About 10 minutes later the phone rang. It was a girlfriend from times past calling. We talked, laughed, and shared. I told her what a pleasure it was to hear from her and asked, "What prompted you to call today?

She replied, "You just crossed my mind, and I thought I would call you right now."

A lot people think that was just a coincidence, but not me. I know it was the Lord answering my pray, as He would do many more times. I was so focused on the loss of romantic love that I lost sight of the fact that I had many friends and family who loved me. I hadn't been in touch. I had lost connection with many of them when my life exploded. After crying out to God, I realized that there was no need to be lonely. I needed only to lift my head to see what was already there. It also illustrated for me that God cares about the even the little things, like, my being lonely.

I have many stories of supernatural help during my season of transformation. Prayer is just a conversation with your higher power. He knows what you are thinking anyway, so you can just be real with him.

Pray **U**ntil **S**omething **H**appens: PUSH is an effective tool when you have done all you can do. Note, I am not advocating to only pray. On the contrary: ***"Pray, but row away from the rocks!"***[xvii]

YOUR NEW LIFE COMPASS

Chapter 4

One More Time

"Our greatest weakness is in giving up. The most certain way to succeed is always to try just one more time."
—Thomas Edison
American inventor

"And you can tune into your purpose, really, align with it, setting goals so that your vision is an expression of that purpose, then life flows much more easily."
—Jack Canfield
Author, politician

"When you align yourself with God's purpose as described in the scripture, something special happens."
—Bono
Lead singer of U2

Action: *Align • Affirm • Authenticate*

ALIGN

If you are reading this book, you are interested in changing your current circumstance for the better. Change in general can be difficult, but it is less difficult when it can be made in small incremental steps. There is no more powerful a person than one aligned to their core values and purpose. Since most of the motivation to move forward with your life transformation will come from within, it is important that you be aligned internally (mind, heart, soul, and spirit). Once I became clear about my purpose, power followed. The two exercises outlined in this chapter are two small steps to take as you get in alignment with your purpose.

Any investigation of purpose includes discernment of your values. So, just what are your core values? If you have not had time to think about your values, or if it's been awhile since you have revisited them, you are not alone. By core values, I am referring to the qualities, characteristics, or principles you hold dear. Your values are what are important to you, and they are uniquely yours. Even if two people happen to choose the same value word, such as "integrity," each person may define it and walk it out differently. Examples of values are honesty, adventure, humor, collaboration, etc. I encourage you to spend a peaceful afternoon exploring your values. I have included a values exercise on the next page. There are no wrong or right answers here. To reference *"A list of Some Universal Needs and Values"* join the ***Girl Get it Right! Action*** FaceBook group.[viii] You can also just brainstorm attributes you would like to exhibit in a life well lived. When we are living aligned to our values, it makes our heart sing. Please carve out time now to discern your values. The answers are inside of you!

Exercise IV Defining Core Values

Identifying and Prioritizing Your Values (Estimated time: 2 hours/ day for 2 days)

The following process can help you identify and prioritize the values that mean the most to you:

- Begin by listing your most important values. You can search the Internet for a list of values, but search within to identify the values that you uniquely own. Write down your 10 most important values, and use clarifying words to flesh out the description of each value.

- Once you list your values, prioritize your top five values by crossing off the values of lesser importance until only five remain. Your degree of discomfort in doing this will reveal the importance of the value. To test the ultimate importance of a value, envision a situation where you cannot honor the value. For example, one of my values is integrity. If my employer asked me to give her a gift that had been donated to the organization's fund-raiser silent auction, I would be uncomfortable with that.

- To help prioritize your values, imagine that you could only carry your five most important values in your boat as you travel down the river of life. The type of boat you envision tells you a lot about your values, too! Which value do you abandon first? Second? Keep throwing your values overboard until you only have one left. What one value can you not live without? Pay particular attention to how you feel when you consider abandoning one of your top values.

- What single value would you like to pass on to your children (or other people's children) as the most important foundation for a wonderful life?[x]

A note about these exercises: We carry many many values and this is perfectly fine. We are just trying to identify the top five, so that they may serve as guideposts in future decision making. Now that you have more awareness of your values and have prioritized your top "must live with" five core values, let's move on to examine your life experiences.

Exercise V: Life Lessons (Time: 4-6 hours of uninterrupted time)

Determining your purpose on this earth is a part of everyone's life journey. It's about time to discern this, especially now that you are in the middle of creating a new reality for yourself! The point of this exercise is to examine and evaluate the experiences that you have already had, understand your spiritual gifts or natural talents, and align these things with your values. These three things (core values, life experiences, gifts or talents) will point you to your purpose.

No one's life is perfect, and we have all had peaks and valleys. If we take the time to look back over the course of our lives we will often notice patterns and lessons.

I am sure there are major life experiences that have shaped you. What are they? There was a lesson in each of them. What did you learn? Examine those experiences in the rear view mirror. Sometimes, it's easier to identify the lessons you learned after the emotion of the experience has dissipated. Journal these things. This is deep stuff and it may be painful to look back and remember. **Isn't is equally painful to repeat mistakes and live uninformed?** Our wisdom from the past can and should inform the steps we take in the future.

Take as long as you need. You may need to do this over a weekend if you have had a long, eventful life. Evaluating your life experiences in the context of your values and gifts/talents are important steps in discerning your purpose.

My Story Circa 2010: *More Meaning, Please*

I spent time revisiting and clarifying my purpose in 2010. On the heels of another HP threat to lay off more staff and offer early retirement, my spirit and purpose led me to do work that was more meaningful to me. At this point, I had been leading a domestic violence ministry through my church since 2002. I felt my life was already purposeful after work.

Crafting my purpose statement was a deliberative process that was significant for me. My purpose statement still holds today. It serves as a guidepost for me as my life takes its twists and turns. With some focused time, I landed my purpose statement: *"To be a beacon to others on the path to living peacefully, joyfully, authentically, and on purpose!"* What's your purpose statement?

Determining your purpose does take effort and time on your part. You can do it on your own. I did. The workbook I used was called Chazown (khaw-ZONE), which is a Hebrew word that means vision, written by Greg Groeshel. He offers a free online version. This book has a Christian orientation and is very structured. It took me two months to get through this process. It was thorough and effective.

If you need help with this, I offer two styles of one-on-one coaching sessions to help you determine your purpose: a Christian version and a secular version. For the secular version, we talk about natural talents as opposed to spiritual gifts. There's no getting around the time commitment though. It will still probably take you two months. My six-session purpose coaching package is available to you at https://guestbrownimpact.com/index.php/booking/

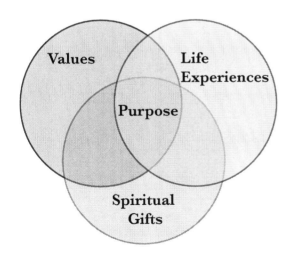

Purpose

Your purpose can be found at the intersection of Values, Spiritual Gifts/Talents and your Life Experience

AFFIRM

"It is the universal need of every human being, from presidents to paupers, to be affirmed."

—Oprah Winfrey

Merriam Webster defines *affirm* as: to assert as true or factual, as a judgment, as valid or confirmed.

Oprah's statement that everyone needs to be affirmed is true. That includes you and me! So, let's be about it. I know Oprah was talking about the external affirmation of others, and sure that feels great, but internal self-validation is even more important.

There are many ways to affirm yourself. Over the years, I have read a number of daily spiritual devotionals that have affirmed that I matter. Those devotionals continue to help me face each day. Among my favorites are: *Our Daily Bread* at ODB.org; *Daily Meditations for People of Color* by Iyanla Vanzant; *Jesus Calling* by Sarah Young; and *The Language of Letting Go* by Melodie Beattie. Even today, I consume a daily affirmation just like a once-a-day vitamin. Just as vitamins supplement the nutritional requirements of the body that you may not get in your food, these affirmations nourish the soul and spirit. My favorite affirmation of all times was the one I created for myself. Join me for the Chapter 4 Facebook discussion on Affirmation to build your affirmation. ***The Girl Get it Right! Action*** Facebook group[ix] is a closed group, available to readers of ***Girl Get it Right!***

My Story Circa 1997: *What Manner of Fresh Hell Awaits Today?*

In 1997, I repeated a simple affirmation in the mirror every morning before facing the day.

My situation was dismal: my soon to be ex-husband was addicted to methamphetamines and threatening to kill himself if I didn't go back to him. I was living separately from him, but he was living in our home, and I was very much connected to his struggles and our joint misery. We were losing our home, our boat, our marriage, and he was no longer working. At this point, he had attacked me in our home and sent me running for safe shelter at a friend's home. I then took a forced semester off from grad school and an extended time off work. I sought counseling, as I waited for my black eye to heal. I was in management at my firm. I was ashamed and pleaded with my closest friends to keep my confidence. The bills piled up. I had anxiety every time I received a bill I could not pay. I had notified the creditors of our impending split, and they called often because they were desperate to go to the top of "bills to be paid" pile. I tried hard to appear normal by going to work and continuing with my studies at grad school. My life was in shambles. I had a colleague who worked in car accident claims, and as she arrived to work each day, she would jokingly say, *"What manner of fresh hell awaits today?"* She had no idea how that statement resonated with me during that time.

During this time, I experienced firsthand the empowerment that comes when you meditate on daily affirmations. My daily affirmations encouraged and grounded me for whatever the day held. Affirmations are a testament to the power of words.

My favorite daily personalized affirmation:

"Gayle, you come from a long line of strong black women. You are educated, smart, hardworking, and resourceful. You have everything you need to do what you need to do right now! If God is for you, who can be against you?"

I repeated this each morning, when looking in the mirror, calling on the strength of my ancestors who had persevered before me, and on my God, who was with me. This worked for me. Only you know what will work for you. I encourage you to craft a personalized affirmation that will strengthen your heart as you do the brave work of changing your life for the better.

Homework: Browse your local bookstore for daily devotionals. Find one that works for you.

To create your own affirmation, join us in the ***Girl Get it Right! Action*** Facebook group to inspire you to get it right. Start today!

https://www.facebook.com/groups/2069591023354323/

AUTHENTICATION

"Authenticity is a collection of choices that we have to make every day. It's about the choice to show up and be real. The choice to be honest. The choice to let our true selves be seen "

—Brené Brown

There is only one you. As someone anonymously and astutely said, *"You might as well be yourself. Everybody else is already taken."* Isn't it incredible that with 7.6 billion people in the world, there's no one quite like you? No one with your unique fingerprint, personality and talents. If you are going to give the world a part of you, let it be the authentic you. In these days of hair and lash extensions, hair weaves, enhanced rear ends, and nails, can we at least be sure our hearts are true? It is so rare to meet an unpretentious heart that you will indeed stand out.

Forgotten who you are at the core? So many people stand with you. Many of us are so involved with caring for others, family, parents, and our job that we have lost contact with who we are and even with what makes our hearts happy. I have coached and talked to many women who appear frozen when I ask, "Setting aside your children and/or your husband, what makes your heart smile?"

Here's a prescription: Revisit old journals, look at old pictures, and interview relatives about your interests at different stages of your life. Reconnect to your authentic self. Live your truth now! It is never too late. We only get one life, so why not live it freely and authentically?

A poem from me to you. Circa 2017

The Authentication of Me:

A more authentic iteration of self

Who Knew?
It would take getting to my second half of life to be truly me!
Truly African American, natural curly haired me,
Truly Gayle, not watered down for public consumption,
Truly me… the real me.
After decades of assimilating to the dominate culture.
Who knew, I would get to this age and come into my own.
To finally accept myself, the way I truly am.
Natural hair
no fake nails or fake lashes.
un-accessorized, unembellished, unbelievably me.
Just me, unadulterated, uncompromisingly Me!
Me, African American me
Me, Christian me
Me, naturally me,
Happily, lovingly me
Authentically me…Finally.

—Gayle Guest-Brown

Communication

Connection

Cultivate

CHAPTER 5

YOU WILL NEED OTHERS
CONNECT AND COMMUNICATE WITH LOVE

"Self-discipline is an act of cultivation. It requires you to connect today's action to tomorrow's results. There is a season for sowing, a season for reaping. Self-discipline tells you which is which."

—Gary Ryan Blair
President of Goals Guy

"Our life is composed greatly from dreams, from the unconscious and they must be brought into connection with action. They must be woven together."

—Anias Nin
French-American novelist

"Reckless words pierce like a sword, but the tongue of the wise brings healing."

Proverbs 17:8

Action: *Cultivate • Connect • Communicate*

CULTIVATE

Here is where you cultivate the change you want to see. By *cultivate*, I mean to tend to or to bring forth your essence. By now you have identified your goals and dreams. As you identify the gaps between where you are now to the desired state of being, brainstorm and capture your ideas. Write them down, so you will remember them later. Water that seed and tend to it. Like any new seed, your dreams will need to be nourished. They will need sun, light, food, and protection from harsh conditions. Limit exposing your dreams to anything that would stand against them.. While appearing dormant on the surface, a new seed is magically germinating, rooting, and sprouting just below the surface.

> *"They thought they buried us*
> *but they didn't know we were seeds."*
> —Dinos Christianopoulos
> Greek poet and author

My Story Circa 2002-2006: *I Knew at the Very Least, I Wanted to Help Others*

As the leader of a domestic violence ministry, I gathered brochures from the local domestic violence service providers. As I went in to pick up brochures from a local provider one day, the training director asked to speak with me. I waited, wondering what this was about. Out walked a tall, honey-colored sister named Shelly Colson. The meeting was pensive. The shelter had trouble with people misrepresenting themselves as their employees. After explaining my purpose she gave me the materials.

Shelly stayed in contact with me over the years. Through the years, she invited me to industry conferences to deepen my knowledge and connection to the field. I was cultivating my knowledge and Shelly was cultivating me. I would go on to serve the field for another twelve years as a volunteer. As I grew in knowledge, I grew in experience. That knowledge and experience would eventually position me to qualify and secure an executive director position at a community domestic violence non-profit service organization. I had been serving the domestic violence community since 2002. Shelly wrote a recommendation letter on my behalf when I applied for the position. At this time, Shelly was the executive director at a sister organization. After I was hired, we continued to cultivate and grow our relationship.

Over thirteen years, I had evolved from a victim to a survivor, to a volunteer, to the head of a domestic violence organization.

Your dreams could unfold more quickly for you, but don't worry about the time; just continue to water and nurture the dream. You are evolving all the time. Be present as much as possible. Our lives are made of thousands of moments along the path, so enjoy them! One day you reach **your** season to reap what you have sown.

CONNECTION

*"One must always maintain one's connection to the past
and yet ceaselessly pull away from it."*
—Gaston Bachelard
French philosopher

*"In my deepest, darkest moments, what really got me
through was a prayer. Sometimes my prayer was, "Help
Me", sometimes a prayer was—"Thank You."
What I've discovered is that intimate connections and
communication with my Creator will always get me
through because I know my support, my help is just a
prayer away."*
—IyanlaVanzant
Inspirational Speaker

Do you Remember those connect-the-dots drawings in elementary school? A page full of numbered dots until you drew a line connecting one dot to the next. Then at last, a recognizable image emerged. Our lives are much like that. The answers (the dots) are often there all the time, but until we sit down to connect the dots in our lives, we do not get the full picture of what is emerging. So, take some time to connect the dots.

- Connect the dots between what you do well naturally (your talents), your spiritual gifts, your core values, and your life experiences to reveal your purpose in life.

- Connect the dots between your acquaintances, your friends, and your family to where you want to end up. This is also known as networking.

- Connect the dots to your belief system and your higher power. This can provide strength, power, and peace beyond all understanding.

Connection is the WD-40 of life. Without it, life can be squeaky and doors can be hard to open. It's time to consider who you know on the path to where you are going. These people are in your life for a reason. Their lives may have evolved to a place that they are now in a position to help someone just like you along the way.

My Story Circa 2016: *Connecting the Dots... Thelma states the obvious*

After three-and-half years in the executive director job, I was contemplating my next step. I had the benefit of an executive leadership coach for a year, conferred as a result of a highly esteemed, 16-month leadership development program. Remember Shelly, my mentor? Yep, she told me about the leadership program, and she recommended me for the next cohort! This was a true blessing. About four months into the program, each of us were able to select a coach to support us. This was a huge benefit for us in the non-profit field. For me personally, it was tremendously helpful to have an outside perspective on issues inside the agency. At the conclusion of the leadership program my coach stated, *"Gayle, you'd make a great leadership coach. You've got all that leadership experience, and you are well connected."* This is what Coaches do. They help you access the wisdom of your lived experiences. Sometimes it's obvious, and sometimes it's obscure. In my case, I was overlooking this possibility and did not see what was right in front of me. I hadn't considered leadership coaching until that time.

I took some time to deliberate about leadership coaching as a next step. After reflecting on of my gifts, values, and experiences, I had to admit it made a lot of sense. Soon, the picture became crystal clear. Eight years earlier, I had crafted my purpose statement: *To be a beacon to others on the path to living peacefully, joyfully, authentically, and on purpose!* Through coaching, speaking, and writing I could live out my purpose and reach a broader audience! My leadership coach stated the obvious and helped me to connect the dots of my life's journey.

So, what is your purpose statement? Why not spend some time with what you already know about yourself and allow some space to consider what you are becoming? At the conclusion of life, what impact do you want to have had? How do you want to be remembered? How do you want to show up? Carve out time each week for a month to think about this and write your purpose statement. To complete this exercise you will need to consider you natural talent or giftings and your skills. For the purposes of this exercise, let's use these definitions of talent and skill by Merriam-Webster:

Talent

1. a: a special often athletic, creative or artistic aptitude

    b: general intelligence or mental power

Skill

1. a: the ability to use one's knowledge effectively and readily in execution or performance

    b: dexterity or coordination especially in the execution of learned physical tasks

2. a: a learned power of doing something competently : a developed aptitude or ability

    //language *skills*

Note for Christians: If you know your spiritual giftings you may choose to use to let that knowledge inform your talent choice. Let's use this definition for spiritual gifts:

Spiritual Gifts: a manifestation or expression from the Holy Spirit in the life of believers which empowers them to serve the body of Christ, the church.[xi]

I have reserved some space on this page for your purpose statement. Try this:

My Purpose Statement
Date:

I want to use my natural ability/ies or spiritual gifts of
_____ and _____
skills to impact _____(what specific population)

I want to use my natural ability/ies or spiritual gifts of
_____ and _____
skills to impact _____(what specific population)

I want to use my natural ability/ies or spiritual gifts of
_____ and _____
skills to impact _____(what specific population)

Example: I want to use my natural abilities of encouraging others and my leadership skills to impact women who are overcoming difficult circumstances.

Note: You will want to date your purpose statement as it may evolve over time. Getting clear about who you are and where you spend your energy will help you to **live life "On Purpose."**

COMMUNICATE

"Communication is to a relationship like oxygen is to life, without it…it dies"

—Tony Gaskin
Motivational speaker

"To Listen well is as powerful a means of communication and influence as to talk well"

—John Marshall
Fourth Chief Justice of the U.S.

We will inevitably find ourselves facing transitions in our careers, relationships, and homes. It's best to be proactive with the messaging around these life events. Managing your own public relations and internal relations takes time and that's okay. As we try on new ways of being, we will need to think about and do things differently. As India Aria says, *"the words from your mouth, you are the first to hear."* So, edify, lift up, speak life and encourage yourself and others about the events of your life. As I left the non-profit executive director job to go into business for myself, I knew I would have to share just enough about the situation to express why I was making a transition. Despite my successes there, the circumstances had become uncomfortable.

My Story Circa July 2016: *Encourage Yourself* – a song by Donald Lawrence.

One of my newest board members had just left my office. As I digested what had happened, it confirmed what I had suspected. I realized the climate at the agency had shifted, and in fact, our board of directors was experiencing a rotation of new officers. I sensed that I may be leaving that job sooner than later. I had already began to do some succession planning for the organization. The loss of an executive director can set an organization back, but there was a slow moving storm brewing, and the board meetings had become less and less collaborative. I could feel this shifting of the winds on many levels. I prayed for direction many times and felt led to stay put.

On this day, the newest board member had arrived just before the board meeting began. He was an older white male of certain age and a different time, and he now spent time volunteering on our board. He was the kind of man that refers to women as "Gals." He thought he was doing me a favor when he advised: *"I think you would get along much better if you were more submissive."* Submissive? My spine straightened, and my head snapped around to meet his eyes. I thought to myself: Are you kidding me? I am the executive director of a domestic violence and sexual assault shelter, and you want me to be more submissive! His eyes were void of emotion, and I could see he meant no harm but he was serious, he really did mean submissive. He was clueless this word has no place in a professional work setting.

All too often, out of desperation to fill board seats, non-profit agencies bring on board members who are not aligned to their mission, culture, or values. The impact of that mismatch is a loss of efficiency and effectiveness. I knew what this signaled and I knew in my heart that I would not be there much longer. There was a limit to how much I would handle. This was it. I had given my all to this agency, but I had no time or energy for adding the burden of tackling race or gender bias (implicit or explicit) to my efforts there. I also knew I would not move without a nod from my God. I would put my best foot forward until I received the okay to move.

Later that month, while walking before work, I received an answer to my prayer, as I listened to Joel Osteen online. He preached that sometimes God makes you uncomfortable to help you step into a higher level of purpose. During that broadcast my phone rang. It was a friend, informing me that there was a position open at her agency closer to my home. I took it as a sign from on high. I had been waiting for this nod. I began to prepare to transition from that job. I also, prepared my letter of resignation.

I committed this scripture to memory: *"Life and death lie in the power of the tongue"* (Proverbs 18:21). The other scripture I leaned on was Psalm 37:1-9 but specifically verses 5-6:

> *"Commit your way to the Lord; trust in him and he will do this: He will make your righteousness shine like the dawn, the justice of your cause like the noon day sun."*

God Was in, and He Was on It!

I was cognizant that what I told myself and others about this experience mattered greatly to my future. I also knew, I did want to harm the agency's reputation or their effectiveness in the community. They were doing the important work of serving victims of domestic violence and it was important to me that work continue.

Years earlier, I found this sage advice in the book *This Is Not the life I Ordered*.[xii] It's a great tool for communicating the shifts in your life.

"When life topples you, it is tempting to share your shock, your dismay, or the unfairness of it all. Well-meaning people will ask you what happened and what you will do now. What you express to others about the experience to others is important to your recovery and redirection. Ask yourself these three questions:

- What's the good in this situation?
- Who can help me?
- What do I say about it?"

I sat down one day to think through the narrative I would share when well-meaning people would ask me what happened or why I left:

"I gave them 3.5 years of my life and accomplished great things for the community. I increased the agency budget by 41 percent in my time there, and I increased the office space, which allowed employees to take a break and eat away from their desks. I am super proud of the new, beautiful shelter we had built on several acres with a pond, a wraparound porch, and even a chandelier. The shelter expanded capacity by 104 percent. The agency is doing important work in the community, but I desired to work closer to home and step into a higher level of my calling."

The fact was, **it was time to leave.** I longed for work that was closer to home, that would allow me to step into a higher level of purpose. I wanted to do work that was replenishing, evergreen, and I found that in executive leadership coaching, training, and speaking. I chose not to focus on the issues that were certainly part of the weariness. I chose to speak life and encouragement.

All of the above were true. The negatives were also true but they would not have served me or the agency. Joyce Meyers, a Christian author, says *"Change your words, change your life."* I say, change your mindset, change your life. Taking the high road helped me to stay positive and focused on the future, not in the past.

Years later, First Lady Michelle Obama's words really resonated with me and affirmed my decision to take the high road. She stated simply: "When they go low, we go high."

Chapter 6

It's Darkest Just Before the Dawn

"Nothing happens until the pain of remaining the same outweighs the pain of change."

—Arthur Burt
Veterinarian, Politician

"How does one become a butterfly? You must want to fly so much that you are willing to give up on being a caterpillar."

—Trina Paulus
Author of *Hope for the Flowers*

"and do not be conformed by this world, but be transformed by the renewing of your mind, so that you may prove what the will of God is, that which is good, acceptable and perfect."

Romans 12:2

Action: *Transition • Transform • Transcend*

TRANSITION

Managing your life transitions requires that you prepare and steady yourself for the uncertainties. There are a plethora of unknowns and many questions to answer in any change of direction. This is when you fall back to your affirmations and hold on to something steady. My rock was my faith. I stepped out in faith. The Bible says you only need faith the size of a mustard seed: the faith that your uncertain future is safe in the hands of an all-knowing God. This tenant of my faith comforted me on many an uncertain day.

I encourage you to try on the new practices and habits that serve you. Transitioning from the old to the new is a necessary step in the transformation you are seeking. Move on toward peace and stability. Remember, you can be invited to chaos, but you don't have to attend.

My Story Circa May 1996: *Happy Mother's Day*

It was Mother's Day, and I didn't care. I didn't want to see anyone—not my mother or my then mother-in law. I was stunned and numbed by the chaos and the struggle of our lives at the time. If you had known me back then, you would have known it was very uncharacteristic of me to not care. I celebrated all the holidays, decorated for them, and looked forward to them. I had holiday sweaters, vests, and earrings. This apathy was atypical and a red flag for me.

This change in my countenance made me realize that the situation with my drug-addicted, bipolar husband was impacting my spirit. A friend had given me a pamphlet about a Codependents Anonymous group. In that same slot in my wallet was a card with info about the local domestic violence support group. I was also considering them for the first time. At that time, I didn't think of myself as a domestic violence victim, but I had to acknowledge there was unpredictable violence in my home. On some subconscious level, I courted the possibility that I might need help and held on to these cards. The manager in me thought our problems were situational. Stress at work would eventually subside and things would return to normal. Instead things accelerated, spiraling out of control like a roller coaster ride that would not end. In reality, I was in denial. I had begun to lock the door to the bedroom when my husband returned home late at night. Those nights after drinking were volatile. Mother's Day was the day I started to transition. I decided that I mattered! My spirit mattered. Iyanla Vanzant once said, *"Take care of your spirit, sometimes that's all you have."*

I knew I was not well. I sought to heal myself and find support. I realized I had an obligation to take care of myself. On that day, my mindset transitioned from surviving to thriving. I took two micro steps. I found a Codependents Anonymous meeting and went through my company's confidential employee assistance program to seek out a therapist.

Your new destiny has a way of providing for you. You just have to trust and believe. Sure, it is easier said than done, but there are so many examples of people who have done just this. The famous example that comes to mind is the most well-known African American woman, Oprah Winfrey. She overcame a great hardship during her childhood to become a billionaire today. She was born to a teenage mother and grew up with her grandmother. Also, beginning at the age of nine, Oprah was molested by her uncle, family friend, and cousin. She eventually had a son at the age of 14, but he died during infancy. Children at school made fun of her, calling her ugly and poor. Despite the obvious struggle that she faced, Oprah persisted to succeed.[xiii] Is it time for transition in your life?

The verb transition means to undergo or cause to undergo a process or period of change. Note the words "process" and "period of change," which means transition can take some undefined time to actually happen. It may not happen overnight. It cannot happen unless you change your mind and change your direction. As Rumi, a Thirteenth Century poet said, you must take first step and…"as you start to walk on the way, the way appears."

> *"Sometimes the smallest step in the right direction ends up being the biggest step of your life. Tip toe if you must, but take the step."*
>
> —Unknown.

TRANSFORM

"Let go of the past and go for the future. Go confidently in the direction of your dreams. Live the life you imagined."

—Henry David Thoreau

Actions cause transformation, new ways of being and seeing, and new practices. Say yes to newness! It takes us away from the tried and true, the old and familiar. Yes, this can be difficult for many of us, but we know that old ways won't open new doors.

My Story Circa 1996: *Trust the Still Quiet Voice Inside, aka the Holy Spirit*

One day I was sitting in church, singing along with the choir and a small voice within said, "Join the choir." It was odd, because I knew I didn't have a strong singing voice. I enjoyed singing to the radio and in the shower but that was the extent of it. Then one day the pianist asked me to consider the choir. I asked immediately, "Do you have to audition?" There were no auditions, so I joined the choir.

The choir director sat me right next to Carol Harmon. She would sing loudly enough for me to catch which key to sing in and answer any questions I had. As God would have it, Carol would do much more. She would become my spiritual big sister as I underwent a significant transformation. Carol modeled healthy Christian womanhood during this time. The lyrics of praise would slowly mend my broken spirit and wounded heart. Singing in the choir gave my soul a voice. Healing was necessary for the transformation to begin. It was never really about singing. It was about healing, receiving a model of Christian womanhood, and forming new wings. It was all about the transformation from the old to the new, resulting in a new and evolved me. A stronger, bolder, more authentic and spiritually grounded iteration of myself.

Many of us no longer trust our instincts. I know that was true for me. My instincts were good, though. I just had a habit of discounting them, as our Western culture leans heavily on tangible evidence and things that can be measured.

Merriam Webster defines **Instinct** as

1. a: natural or inherent aptitude, impulse, or capacity

    // had an instinct for the right word

2. a: a largely inheritable and unalterable tendency of an organism to make a complex and specific response to environmental stimuli with out involving reason

    b: behavior that is mediated by reactions below the conscious level

You may not have the benefit of a still quiet voice to guide you, but you have instincts. You can see by the definition here, it's not the same as the Holy Spirit, but you can at least increase your awareness of your natural instincts to be an aid to you. My ask is that you become more aware of your instincts and develop trust in listening to them. I invite you to journal when your instincts are good and where they fail you. Once you have documented that your instincts are working for you, it will give you more confidence about listening to your instincts.

If you are a Christian, you have your instinct and the additional and supernatural guidance of the Holy Spirit. Merriam-Webster defines the Holy Spirit as: the third person of the Christian Trinity. This is consistent with my faith tradition. We believe the Spirit lives within us. We need only to head its nudges.

My ask is that you listen to the urging of the Spirit within. I invite you to journal what happens when you follow the urging of the Holy Spirit and when you do not. Once you have documented that the Holy Spirit is working on your behalf, it will give you more confidence about listening to this internal guide and it will increase your capacity to recognize his voice. In listening and heeding the guidance of the Holy Spirit, you have the assurance that you are walking in the will of God. How cool is that! It gives you even more confidence to move boldly into your future.

TRANSCEND

"Therefore, if anyone is in Christ, he is a new creature, the old things have passed away, behold, new things have come"

2 Corinthian 5:17

Once the butterfly breaks free from the chrysalis (sometimes mistakenly called a cocoon) and takes flight, it has transcended. It is quite a journey from crawling, transforming in the chrysalis, to transcending and taking flight. A butterfly literally takes on new ways of being. A butterfly's once slow-moving, earthbound life now flutters on a gentle breeze. In the same way, we can create an elevated life by crawling, believing, taking action, persisting, and transforming. When we adopt new ways of being, we can transcend our valleys and transform our lives.

My Story Circa 1997 -2018: *"God Favored Me,"* a song by Hezekiah Walker

When I walked away from my ten-year marriage, I wanted to and believed I could first heal and recreate a better life for myself. I first grieved and mourned my broken dreams for that marriage. At the time, it didn't make sense to me that I would ever remarry. I could not have known that my best days were yet to come!

I loved my seven years of freedom as a single woman. I was in a new career as a financial analyst; recovering financially and emotionally, traveling with girlfriends, owning my own home, and making decisions for my life without having to compromise. It was a period of getting to know and appreciate myself. It was an amazing time of growth and discovery.

Fast forward 20 years, and I am now wonderfully remarried to a man of God and character who loves me and honors me. Fourteen years in, and we are still very much in love, and we go skiing and salsa dancing often. My home is warm, peaceful, welcoming, and aesthetically pleasing. My garden, my family, and my friends bring me much joy; my soul is content; my Spirit is anchored in Jesus. I am doing work that helps others and replenishes me.

I didn't know all that I know now when I started in those uncertain first days and years. I am sharing what worked for me. I believe these steps will also work for you, if you work them. YOU are the key to changing your life and you can do it! You must take action. With these three impactful actions in each chapter, you can have the life, love, and work of your dreams. For me, it all started with the first step toward freedom in 1996. Start your journey today! *Girl Get it Right!*

Imagine • Initiate • Illuminate

Meditate • Move • Manifest

Plan • Prepare • Premeditate • P.U.S.H.

Align • Affirm • Authenticate

Cultivate • Communicate • Connect

Transition • Transform • Transcend

Victoria N. Retter

CLOSING

Know that I am in your corner, and I am pulling for you. You can have the life of your dreams! I know it's not easy to reorder, rearrange, and reset your mind, AND I hope you will use the actions outlined in this book to move forward anyway. It is not easy, but it is worth it! Let me share this inspiration from nature about beginning again.

Quaking Aspen trees have a system of roots that grow underground for years and they spread out significantly. When a fire comes, it wipes out the existing trees. The sunlight warms the ground, enabling new life to spring forward from the existing root system. There is a grove in Utah where the root system is estimated to be 80,000 years old, and it occupies 106 acres and contains 47,000 trees!

Darkness doesn't mean lifelessness. Life may be dormant and inactive for a time, as it waits for the proper conditions, temperature, and oxygen to sprout, grow, and thrive.

Open the curtains, let the sun warm you, and grow you. Put on your shades and get ready to shine. Get ready to thrive! It is all so very doable and possible. I did it, and so can you!

I invite you to join a closed Facebook group of readers just like yourself who simply want more. Request to join at. *Girl Get it Right! Action* Facebook group: https://www.facebook.com/groups/2069591023354323/ Here you will find a supportive community to help encourage you along your journey. I look forward to meeting you there.

Girl, Get it Right!

What will you do next? It's your move. Start your journey today!

ENDNOTES

i   *Brick House,* Commodores, Sony/ATV Music Publishing LLC

ii   *The Soul of a Butterfly: Reflections on Life's Journey,* Muhammad Ali,

iii   *Economic Warfare: Secrets of Wealth Creation in the Age of Welfare Politics,* Ziad K. Abdelnour,

iv   *"The power of imagination is the ultimate creative power. no doubt about that. While knowledge defines all we currently know and understand imagination points to all we might yet discover and create. Imagination is more important than knowledge. Your imagination is your preview of life's coming attractions,"* Albert Einstein

v   *"Rainbow in the Cloud: The Wisdom and Spirit of Maya Angelou,"* Maya Angelou, Random House, 2014

vi   *"7 Scientifically Proven Benefits of Gratitude That Will Motivate You to Give Thanks Year-Round,"* Amy Morin, Forbes No. 23, 2014

vii   *The Gift of Silence: The nourishment Your Brain Is Craving,* Patti Clark, Thrive Global, Jan 9, 2017

viii   *This is Not the Life I Ordred, 50 Ways to Keep Your Head Above Water When Life Keeps Dragging You Down,* Deborah Collins Stephens [et al], Canari Press, 2007

ix   Girl Get it Right FaceBook Group, https://www.facebook.com/groups/2069591023354323/

x   *Coaching for Transformation,* Second Edition, Martha Lasley, Virginia Kellogg, Richard Michaels, Sharon Brown, Discover Press, 2015

xi   *Jesus on Leadership: Becoming a Servant Leader,* GeneWilkes, LifeWay

xii   *This is Not the Life I Ordred, 50 Ways to Keep Your Head Above Water When Life Keeps Dragging You Down,* Deborah Collins Stephens [et al], Canari Press, 2007

xiii   *Women of Color Who Succeed Against All Odds,* Americans Perspective, June 5, 2015

ABOUT THE AUTHOR

Gayle Guest-Brown, MBA, PMP, CPC,

Executive Leadership Coach, Trainer and Speaker

Gayle Guest-Brown is a national speaker, leadership coach, and the CEO of Guest Brown impact. She is a certified professional coach (CPC) empowering leaders to access their strengths, connect to their values, and reach their best strategies and solutions. Gayle delivers one-on-one confidential and customized leadership coaching in three, six and twelve-month packages as well as workshops and retreats

Gayle holds an MBA, a project management credential (PMP), and many years of experience at global Fortune 100 businesses successfully motivating people and maximizing project potential. With 30 plus years of success serving the leadership needs of corporate, tech, non-profit, and faith-based organizations, Gayle is well positioned to assist other leaders.

In 2012, Gayle was honored by the Sacramento Cultural Hub and received its Exceptional Women of Color award for her service and community work as founder and Program Manager of *From Bruised and Battered to Blessed Ministries*. You can reach Gayle for speaking, coaching and Training at:

 Guest Brown **impact**   guestbrownimpact.com

 Linkedin.com/in/guestbrownimpact

 facebook.com/ggbcoaching/

Let's Stay Connected!

I would love to hear your stories as you apply these ideas, actions, and strategies to your life. Please take time now to connect with me and others on the path to creating the life and work they dream of on Facebook at the closed ***Girl Get It Right! Action*** Facebook Group.

https://www.facebook.com/groups/2069591023354323

The passcode for our ***Girl Get it Right! Action*** Facebook page is: Action!

73505186R00052

Made in the USA
Columbia, SC
04 September 2019